Kalmus Orchestra Library

JEAN

SIBELIUS

HUMORESQUE No. 4

in G Minor

Edited and Revised by Julia A. Burt

Op. 89b

FULL SCORE

EDWIN F. KALMUS, CO.

INSTRUMENTATION

Solo Violin

Strings

Duration: approx. 4 minutes

PROGRAM NOTE

Jean Sibelius (1865-1957) clearly enjoyed writing the six humoresques for violin and orchestra in 1916-1917. They were not performed until 24th November 1919 together with the first performance of the final version of the fifth symphony. The soloist for the Humoresques was Paul Cherkassky. According to the critics, he came close to being drowned out by the orchestra. This publication is the first quality reprint edition of the *Humoresque No. 4* in G minor.

HUMORESQUE IV

Jean Sibelius, Op. 89b
Edited and revised by Julia A. Burt

EDWIN F. KALMUS & CO., INC.

Selected String Orchestra Publications

FULL ENSEMBLE WORKS

ARENSKY, ANTON STEPANOVICH
A100002   Variations on a Theme of Tchaikovsky, Op. 35a

BARTOK, BELA
Darvas, Gabor
A802890   Dances of Transylvania: Sonatina, Sz. 55

ELGAR, EDWARD
A724390   Sospiri, Op. 70 Adagio

GRAINGER, PERCY ALDRIDGE
A609690   Molly on the Shore, Irish Reel from British Folk Music
Settings, No. 1

GRIEG, EDVARD
A104202   Holberg Suite, Op. 40 (Aus Holbergs Zeit)

HOLST, GUSTAV
A826902   St. Paul's Suite for String Orchestra, Op. 29/2; H118 (Grade 4)

Gustav Holst served as the Director of Music at St. Paul's Girls' School in Hammersmith, London between 1905 and 1934. Originally titled Suite in C, Holst's St. Paul's Suite was one of many pieces the composer wrote for his students. A beautiful and powerful symphonic treatment of English folk tunes, St. Paul's Suite consists of four movements: an energetic Jig, Ostinato, based upon a simple theme, Intermezzo, a rhythmic dance and the Finale, wherein Holst masterfully weaves together the 16th century English dance tune, The Dargason, with the traditional melody, Greensleeves. Although the piece was completed in 1913, it was not published until 1922, due to revisions.

JANACEK, LEOS
A761002   Idyll for Strings

MENDELSSOHN, FELIX
Wolff, Hellmuth Christian
A775002   Sinfonia No. 10: String Symphony in B minor

A774390   Sinfonia No. 3: String Symphony in E minor

MOZART, WOLFGANG AMADEUS
A105202   Eine kleine Nachtmusik (Serenade in G), K. 525

A105602   Three Divertimenti, K. 136-138/125a-c (Salzburg Symphony
Nos. 1-3)

REINECKE, CARL
A702002   Serenade in G minor, Op. 242

SHOSTAKOVICH, DMITRI
Drew, Lucas
A584302   Sinfonia (Symphony) for String Orchestra from String Quartet
No.8, Op.110

Dmitri Shostakovich's String Quartet No. 8 in C minor, Opus 110 is dedicated to "The Memory of the Victims of Fascism and War." The work was composed in three days during July, 1960. The Quartet is autobiographical and uses themes from earlier works. The opening theme is an adaption of the composer's name to German sounds: (D-S-C-H). This string orchestra version enhances the deep emotion of this significant work of Shostakovich. The integrity of the phrasing and articulation of the urtext edition has been respected in this edition of Shostakovich's Quartet No. 8.

SHOSTAKOVICH, DMITRI
Gosman, Lazar
A781290   Four Preludes from Op. 34

A781190   Spanish Dance, D. 580

Spanish Dance is an excerpt from Shostakovich's 1955 film score for "The Gadfly." The Soviet movie was based on the eponymous novel by Irish novelist Ethel Lilian Voynich. This arrangement for string orchestra was written by Lazar Gosman.

SIBELIUS, JEAN
A570290   Andante Festivo, Op. 117a

SIBELIUS, JEAN
Drew, Lucas
A810602   String Quartet, Op. 4: Presto (composer's transcription)
Scandinavian

STRAUSS II, JOHANN
A665890   Pizzicato Polka

SUK, JOSEF
A107902   Serenade, Op. 6

SVENDSEN, JOHAN SEVERIN
A326690   Two Swedish Folk Melodies, Op. 27

TCHAIKOVSKY, PETER
A726290   Elegie in G Major

A108502   Serenade in C, Op. 48

The premiere of Tchaikovsky's *Serenade* was conducted by the composer himself in Saint Petersburg on February 8, 1908. The score is dedicated to Sergei Taneyev, a Russian composer, teacher, theorist, author, and pupil of Tchaikovsky. Alongside his Piano Concertos Nos. 2 and 3, this work remains one of the composer's best-known compositions.

TCHAIKOVSKY, PETER
Gosman, Lazar
A006490   Serenade in C, Op. 48

WIREN, DAG IVAR
A797702   Serenade, Op. 11

This spirited work for string orchestra is the best-known composition from 20th-century Swedish composer Dag Wiren. Written in 1937, Serenade for Strings features four contrasting movements: I. Preludium, II. Andante espressivo, III. Scherzo, IV. Marcia.

SOLO BRASS WITH ENSEMBLE

GRAINGER, PERCY ALDRIDGE
A675390   Irish Tune from County Derry: British Folk Music Settings, No.
15

SOLO KEYBOARD WITH ENSEMBLE

ANDERSON, LEROY
A908190   Fiddle-Faddle

An American Pops classic in it's original scoring, this work is part of the Anderson Classics Series by E.F. Kalmus.

SOLO STRINGS WITH ENSEMBLE

ELGAR, EDWARD
A103002   Introduction and Allegro, Op. 47

HANDEL, GEORGE FRIDERIC
Seiffert, Max
A115402   Concerto Grosso in D, Op. 6 No. 5, HWV 323

MENDELSSOHN, FELIX
Unger, Renate
A773902   Concerto for Violin in D minor (2nd version)

VAUGHAN WILLIAMS, RALPH
A819102   Fantasia on a Theme by Thomas Tallis

Original edition of Vaughn William's 1910 work, scored for expanded string orchestra and solo string quartet.

Exclusively Distributed by

Alfred Music
LEARN · TEACH · PLAY

Questions/ comments? info@keiserproductions.com